**W9-DDA-734**

GEM STONES

Designed and produced by
Aladdin Books Ltd
70 Old Compton Street
London W1

First published in the
United States in 1987 by
Gloucester Press
387 Park Avenue South
New York, NY 10016

ISBN 0-531-17057-8

Library of Congress Catalog
Card Number: 87-80463

Printed in Belgium

Design   David West
              Children's Book Design
Editor   Margaret Fagan
Researcher   Cecilia Weston-Baker
Illustrator   Louise Nevett
Consultant   Alan Jobbins

CONTENTS

GEM STONES

Ian Mercer

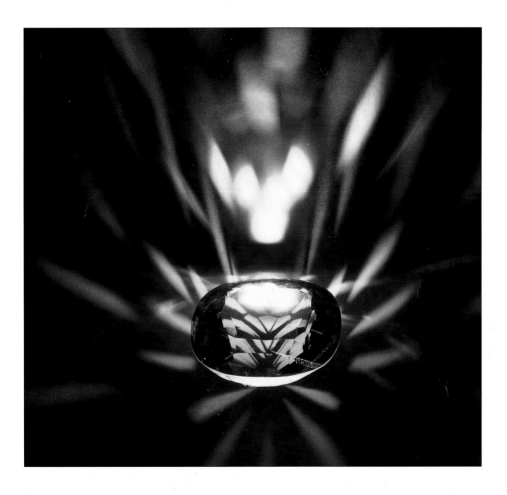

GLOUCESTER PRESS
New York · London · Toronto · Sydney

WHAT IS A GEMSTONE?

Usually when we think of gemstones we imagine a jeweler's shop window. Or we imagine a beautiful ring or necklace. The diamonds, rubies and other gems in these jewels are crystals which have been cut up and polished. Gemstones are made from rare crystals which are hard and clear, or colorful. They are extremely valuable because of their beauty and rarity. But hard or clear crystals are not only used to make jewelry, they are also used in factories, spacecraft and lasers.

Polished gemstones are set into jewelry

Crystals in the Earth's rocks are called minerals. Gems made from minerals are called natural gemstones. Artificial gemstones are made from glass (these are called "paste") and from crystals made in laboratories and factories. Gems of all kinds are often made in order to imitate more valuable gemstones. In this book you will discover the ways hard crystals are formed, how they are processed and how they are used in industry and in jewels.

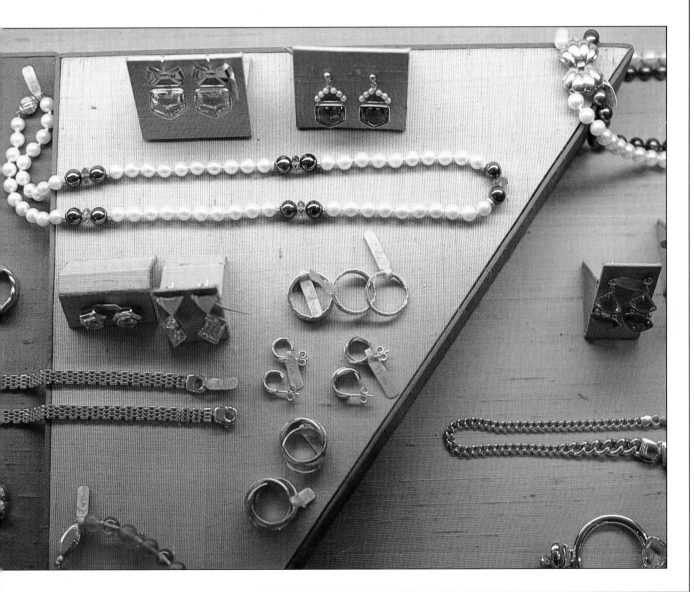

GEMS FROM THE EARTH

The Earth's crystal rocks are moving, squashing together and often melting together. In this turmoil, gems are formed.

In fact, the Earth's rocks are a mixture of minerals which are themselves made up of chemical elements. Atoms of chemical elements, such as carbon, oxygen and silicon, join up to make tiny building blocks which fit together in neat regular patterns to form "crystals."

Natural gems are found as clear or colored crystals embedded in rock. They are also found as big crystals lining cracks or cavities in the Earth's surface layer, or "crust." The rocks and gems are carried away by rivers as they wear down the land. These gem minerals, because they are hard and heavy, can survive the rough journey and may eventually be picked out of the sand and gravel at the surface.

How gems are formed
Some gem crystals, like garnet, grow in solid rock as it squashes beneath moving mountains (1). Others, such as tourmaline, are formed in veins beneath the earth's surface (2).

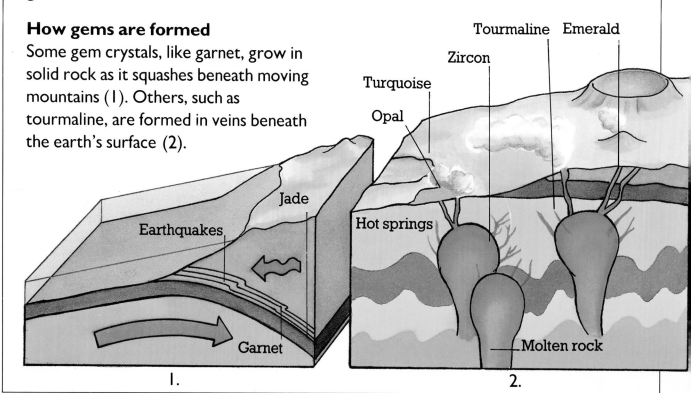

1.

2.

6

An emerald crystal as it appears in rock

Stones such as agate grow in volcanic rocks at the surface (3).
Gems like ruby grow deep down where molten rock "cooks" the Earth's crust. Diamond crystals grow way down beneath the crust (4).

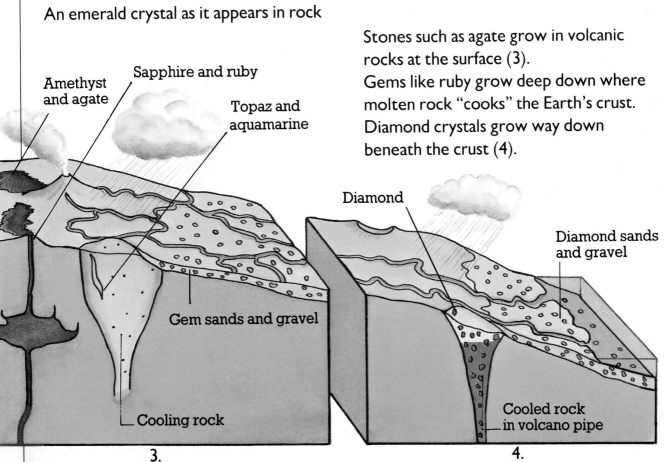

Amethyst and agate

Sapphire and ruby

Topaz and aquamarine

Gem sands and gravel

Cooling rock

3.

Diamond

Diamond sands and gravel

Cooled rock in volcano pipe

4.

MINING FOR GEMS

Most diamonds come from very big and deep mines. Often the mines are in the underground "pipes" of extinct volcanoes. First the top rocks are removed to make a pit. Then huge shafts are driven beneath the open pit. On the southwest coast of Africa, another type of diamond mining takes place. There diamonds lie buried in an ancient pebble beach now covered by huge sand dunes. Over 66 million tons of sand and pebbles have to be removed to extract half a ton of diamonds.

Gems like opal, topaz and emerald mostly come from very small tunnels or gravel pits close to the Earth's surface. "Dirt" is scooped out of the pit, washed and sieved, and any gems are hand-picked from the sieve.

Some mines are extremely deep. You can see one of the mining levels in this big diamond mine (1). Huge cones are cut out of the solid rock so that shattered rock falls through onto railway trucks running through a tunnel.

Australian opal miners actually live inside mines (2). It takes a lot of work to free the gems from very hard rock. People search the dumps hoping to find those opals they may have overlooked!

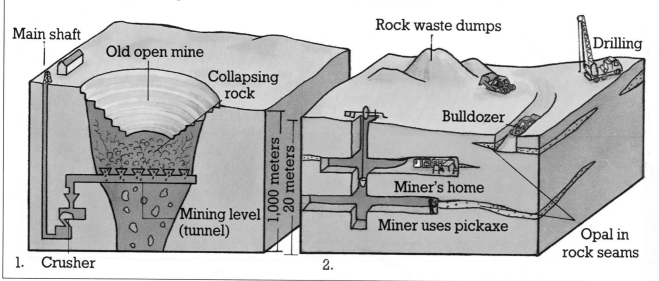

Main shaft
Old open mine
Collapsing rock
Mining level (tunnel)
1,000 meters
20 meters
1.   Crusher

Rock waste dumps
Drilling
Bulldozer
Miner's home
Miner uses pickaxe
Opal in rock seams
2.

8

Mining for gems in a huge diamond mine, South Africa

Working an open gem mine in Kampuchea

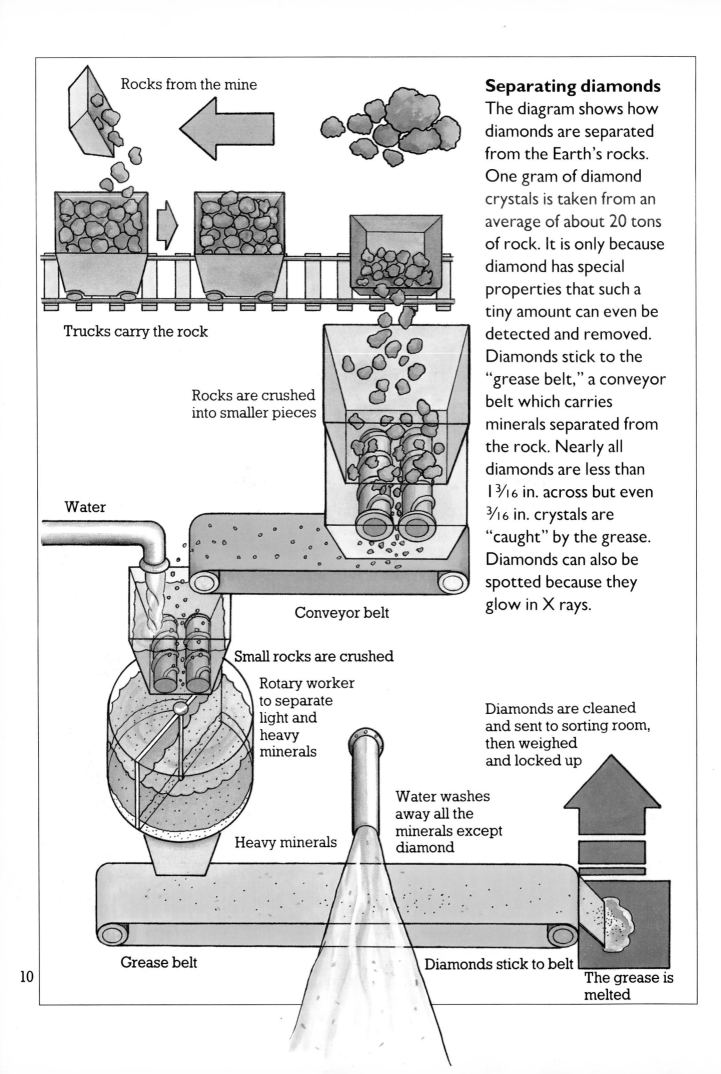

Rocks from the mine

Trucks carry the rock

Rocks are crushed into smaller pieces

Water

Conveyor belt

Small rocks are crushed

Rotary worker to separate light and heavy minerals

Heavy minerals

Grease belt

Separating diamonds
The diagram shows how diamonds are separated from the Earth's rocks. One gram of diamond crystals is taken from an average of about 20 tons of rock. It is only because diamond has special properties that such a tiny amount can even be detected and removed. Diamonds stick to the "grease belt," a conveyor belt which carries minerals separated from the rock. Nearly all diamonds are less than 1 3/16 in. across but even 3/16 in. crystals are "caught" by the grease. Diamonds can also be spotted because they glow in X rays.

Diamonds are cleaned and sent to sorting room, then weighed and locked up

Water washes away all the minerals except diamond

Diamonds stick to belt

The grease is melted

10

SORTING DIAMONDS

Diamonds from the mine are sorted into two groups, industrial and gem quality. Many of the stones are brown or full of bits of mineral which reduce their value and make them unsuitable for jewelry. Gem quality diamonds are sorted according to their weight, color, clarity and shape.

Every year over 13 tons of diamonds are mined but only a small amount is of gem quality. The rest are industrial diamonds. These are worn down through use, so they always have to be replaced and therefore demand is high.

The world's supply and prices of diamonds are very carefully controlled. Dealers and cutters go to "sights" to view small packets of the stones.

One week's production of diamonds from a large mine

SHAPING DIAMONDS

A diamond can be cut and shaped only by another diamond. Each diamond crystal can only be cut in certain directions, along which it is a little less hard. Even so, it takes hours to saw through a diamond. Diamonds can also be split, or "cleaved," along four different directions through the crystal.

Nearly all diamonds are "brilliant cut." This means that the facets – faces of the gems – are cut at just the correct angles to make the most of a diamond's glittering "fire," or sparkle. Each facet acts like a polished mirror inside the gem – it reflects the light while it is split into the colors of the rainbow.

There are several different stages involved in shaping a diamond crystal into a cut gem. First the crystals are sent to special factories and sawed with thin bronze disks coated in diamond dust and olive oil (1). The designer decides where each crystal is to be sawed. Then each diamond is "bruted," or shaped (2). The bruter shapes the gem by holding another diamond against it while it is spun around at great speed. After grinding and smoothing the top facet or "table," the cutter carefully decides where to grind the first of the 16 main facets. When the main facets are polished to the right size (3), the "brillianteer" grinds the other 40 small facets. Over half of the original crystal has now been cut or ground away! Yet every speck is saved.

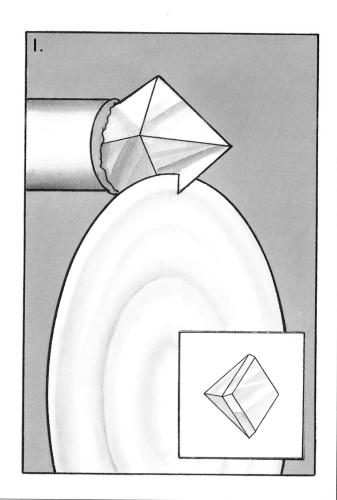

Bruting a diamond with another diamond

2.

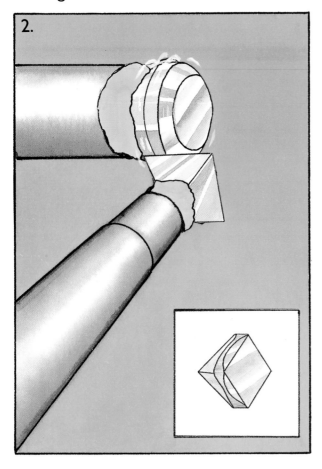

3.

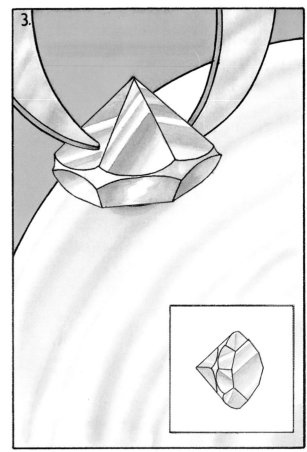

13

SHAPING GEMS

There are many ways of shaping, or "cutting" a gemstone. A person who cuts gems is called a "lapidary." The type of cut is chosen which best displays the color, sparkle, sheen, or some other beautiful optical effect. Gems are sliced with diamond saws and ground into flat facets or curved surfaces. Then they are polished with diamond or ruby powder.

Many clear gems are cut with flat, mirror-like facets. Their angles are carefully set to allow for the way that the light "bends" as it enters and leaves the gem. Each kind of gem has its own special set of facet angles: brilliant cut ruby has different angles from topaz, for instance. A faceted gem will twinkle or show its color well only if it has been cut with correct facet angles.

The different types of cut

The "emerald cut" is oblong with the corners cut off. Long facets send lots of light back from deeply colored, transparent gems. Some gems are carved so that little scenes, symbols or figureheads stand out. These are called "cameos." "Cabochons" are gems which have been cut in the shape of a dome. This type of cut shows off bright colors in opaque gems – gems which do not let light through. Cabochons are also made to reveal beautiful tricks of light, such as "stars" in certain rubies and sapphires, the sheen in moonstones, colors in opals and the bright line which can be seen inside the rare, honey-colored "cat's eye" gems.

Simple cabochon

Double cabochon

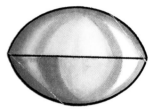

Hollow cabochon

Opals are often cut into cabochons

15

ARTIFICIAL GEMS

We have seen how crystals are made up of atoms fitted together in regular patterns. These patterns can be made to change – with dramatic results. Black graphite is made of carbon atoms; diamond is also made up of carbon atoms but arranged in a different pattern. By applying huge amounts of pressure the carbon atoms in black graphite can be squeezed together to make the more compact diamond pattern. This process however is only used to make industrial quality diamonds. It would be too expensive to use this process to make a diamond large enough to be set into a ring.

A hard, sparkling, artificial substance called CZ is made into gems which look just like diamond. CZ gems are far cheaper than diamonds.

Ruby and sapphire furnace

Artificial crystals are made in furnaces like the one in the diagram. Rows of these furnaces make clear, sausage-shaped crystal rods of ruby or sapphire. These are cut in great numbers to make very inexpensive gems. Other kinds of furnaces are used for making perfect crystals used in lasers. CZ crystal is made in special furnaces at more than 2,500°C (4,532°F).

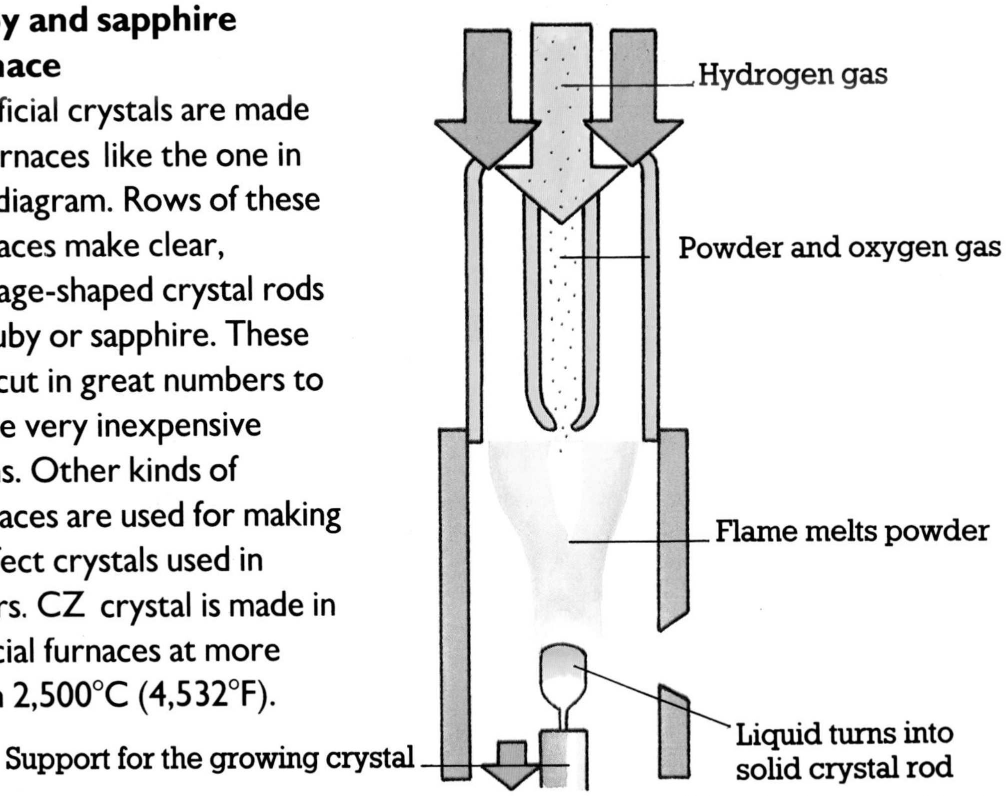

Hydrogen gas

Powder and oxygen gas

Flame melts powder

Liquid turns into solid crystal rod

Support for the growing crystal

A selection of artificial gems – showing the crystal rod shapes

IS IT REAL?

Some kinds of gems are made as imitations of more valuable gemstones. Often, cheaper natural gems which look similar are used. For example, citrine looks like the more costly topaz. Sometimes, however, artificial gems are used. These are not always made of the same substance as the gem they are imitating: CZ imitates diamond which is far more expensive.

Different gems can also be put together in a way that can deceive you – as the diagram shows. "Gemologists" test gems and crystals to find out exactly what they are made of. They have to look closely inside the gem through a lens or microscope. They also test the quality of light coming out of a gem and can tell whether the sapphire (right) is artificial or natural.

Gemstone "tricks" to watch out for

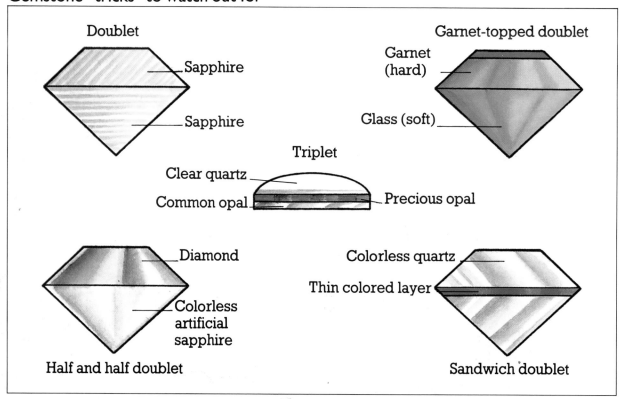

Doublet
Sapphire
Sapphire

Garnet-topped doublet
Garnet (hard)
Glass (soft)

Triplet
Clear quartz
Common opal
Precious opal

Diamond
Colorless artificial sapphire
Half and half doublet

Colorless quartz
Thin colored layer
Sandwich doublet

Light coming through the facets of a natural sapphire — magnified 50 times

DIAMONDS IN INDUSTRY

Diamond is far harder than any other natural substance and can cut through anything. For this reason it has many uses in industry. For example, diamond powder is used for polishing lenses and gems and for sawing tiny silicon wafers to make chips for computers. Most diamond powder is artificially produced.

Diamond "grit" is used for shaping hard metal and ceramic tools, grinding lenses and gems, and in drills used to make holes in stone and concrete. A lot of fine diamond grit is made artificially.

Whole "stones" are used for cutting and engraving glass, making grinding wheels perfectly level, as teeth in large saws for slicing building stone and as drills powerful enough to cut holes in highways. They are also set into the drills of oil and gas wells exploring underneath the sea bed.

A diamond saw being used to "slice" through a highway

A diamond drilling bit

Oil rigs often use diamond bits to drill beneath the sea bed

PRECISION INSTRUMENTS

Artificial quartz is often used in precision instruments. Electric pulses sent through a specially cut quartz plate will make the plate "hum" at one exact and very high-pitched note. This exact vibration is used as the beat to keep time in a "quartz" clock or watch. Tiny "jewel" bearings, often rubies, are fitted inside clockwork watches. They are used because their hard surfaces are not worn away by the workings of the watch.

High-quality natural diamonds are used to make fine scalpel blades for surgeons to use in delicate eye operations. The precision-made stylus in a record player pick-up is a diamond and therefore lasts for a long time. Heat flows through diamond very easily, so tiny diamond pieces are used in television transmitters to keep electronic devices cool.

A quartz watch
Like a quartz plate, a slab of gelatin will wobble at an exact rate, keeping time with a certain beat of the spoon. In your watch, a battery supplies electric pulses to "wobble" the quartz to create a steady pulse.

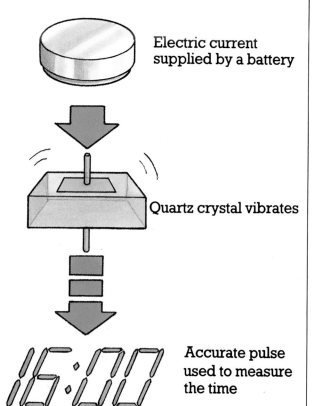

Electric current supplied by a battery

Quartz crystal vibrates

Accurate pulse used to measure the time

The workings of a 17-jewel clock

An electron microscope photograph of a diamond stylus in a record groove

GEMS IN SPACE AND MEDICINE

Many artificial substances are used in laser and electronic research. Some of these substances can be made into crystals which are very pure. Because they are very hard, they also make fine gemstones. CZ, the best diamond imitation, is one example. It was first sold in 1976 after scientists had successfully made it into large size crystals. Lasers with gem-quality crystal rods are used in hospitals. For example, one kind is used to treat injured eyes.

Diamond has many special properties. It is transparent to many kinds of radiation and it can withstand huge pressures. This makes it suitable for use in space, and in weather and spy satellites. A special window was made from a perfect diamond for the 1978 Pioneer space probe to Venus.

The diamond window (center) of the Venus probe

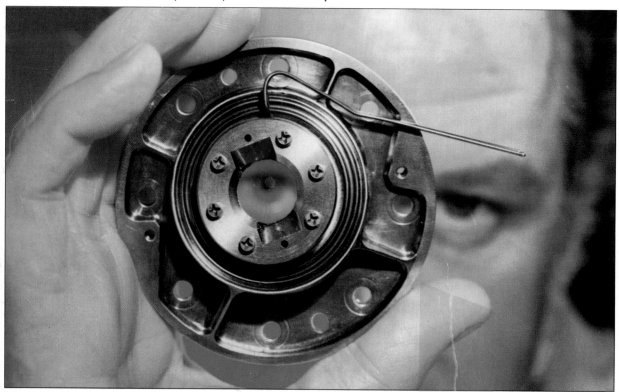

An electron microscope photograph of the diamond chips on a dental drill

THE STORY OF A DIAMOND RING

2. THE MINERALS ARE POURED ON A GREASE BELT. ONLY DIAMONDS STICK ON AND ARE SCRAPED OFF.

1. IN DEEP MINES, POWERFUL DIAMOND DRILLS MAKE HOLES FOR EXPLOSIVES TO BREAK THE ROCK. HEAVY MINERALS ARE SEPARATED FROM THE CRUSHED ROCK.

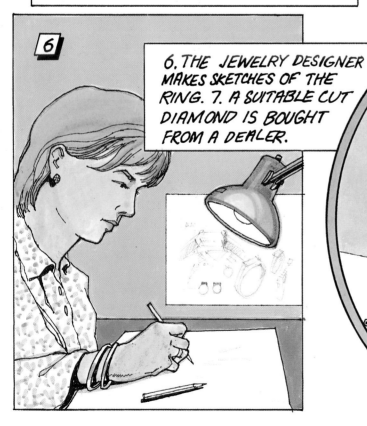

6. THE JEWELRY DESIGNER MAKES SKETCHES OF THE RING. 7. A SUITABLE CUT DIAMOND IS BOUGHT FROM A DEALER.

3. THE DIAMONDS ARE SORTED. SOME ARE LARGE AND CLEAR. IF THEY ARE THE RIGHT SHAPE AND COLOR THEY ARE CLASSIFIED AS GEMS.

4. THE DIAMONDS ARE SENT TO ALL PARTS OF THE WORLD FOR CUTTING AND SHAPING.

5. INDUSTRIAL DIAMONDS ARE USED TO CUT AND SHAPE THE GEMSTONES.

8. THE GOLD RING IS SHAPED AND A HALLMARK IS STAMPED ON TO GUARANTEE THE PURITY OF THE GOLD. THE DIAMOND IS SET INTO THE RING AND POLISHED READY FOR THE JEWELER'S SHOWCASE.

27

The map shows where the world's gems are mined. The diamond mines produce both gem-quality and industrial diamonds. The gem-quality diamond trade is separate from the rest of the diamond trade. Although most of the diamonds sold are industrial diamonds, the value of the gem diamond trade is much greater. This is because of the much higher value of gem diamonds. The map also shows where artificial diamonds are made for use in industry. The world's largest diamond mines are in South Africa. Most artificial diamonds are produced in the United States. Only a total of 286 tons of diamond have ever been separated from the Earth's rocks in the whole history of diamond mining. The world's total of all gem, industrial, natural and synthetic diamond is 52 tons per year. Most of this (44 tons) is tiny industrial diamonds called "abrasives." Large rubies and emeralds are more valuable than colorless diamonds of the same size. Pretty, colored diamonds are very rare and valuable, however.

The world's famous diamonds

The Star of Africa is the world's largest cut diamond. It was cut from the biggest diamond ever found and is included in the British Crown Jewels. The Smithsonian pink diamond, although small, is extremely valuable because of its unusual color.

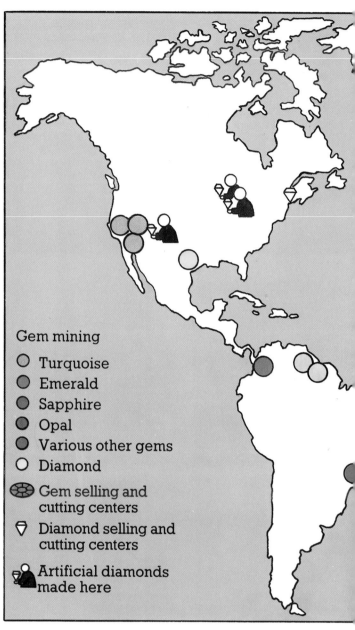

Gem mining

- ◯ Turquoise
- ⬤ Emerald
- ⬤ Sapphire
- ⬤ Opal
- ⬤ Various other gems
- ◯ Diamond
- ⊕ Gem selling and cutting centers
- ▽ Diamond selling and cutting centers
- Artificial diamonds made here

Green Dresden
41 carats

Star of Africa
530.20 carats

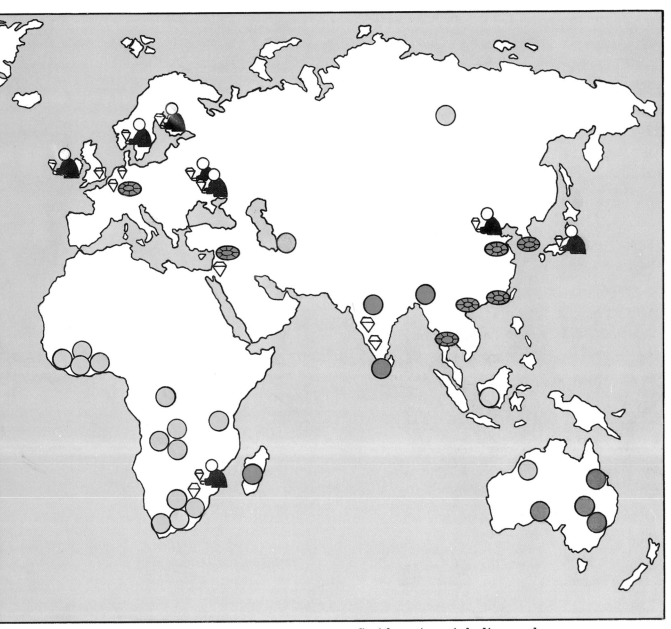

Tiffany yellow diamond
128 carats

Smithsonian pink diamond
2.9 carats

Eugénie blue diamond
33 carats

Black Amsterdam diamond
33 carats

Blue hope diamond
44.5 carats

Enlargement

FACT FILE 2

Weighing gemstones

Diamonds and other gemstones are weighed in a special unit. This is called a "carat." There are five carats (cts) in one gram. Therefore 1kg is 5,000 cts. Tiny diamonds have their own measure. They are weighed in "points." One carat is 100 points, so a quarter-carat gem (0.25 ct) is a "twenty-five pointer." Gold is also measured in carats but these are not based on weight. They are amounts of gold in metal, and 24 carats is equivalent to 100 per cent pure gold. The diagram compares the sizes of diamonds.

Comparing the sizes in diamonds using their carat values

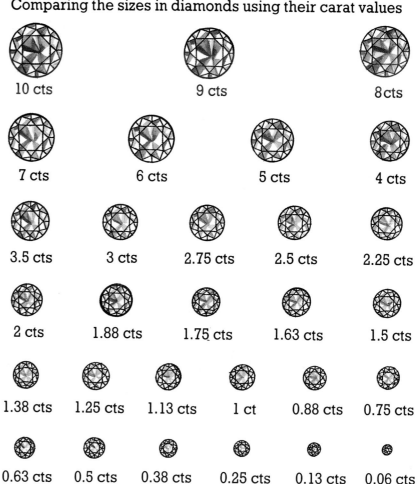

| 10 cts | 9 cts | 8cts |

| 7 cts | 6 cts | 5 cts | 4 cts |

| 3.5 cts | 3 cts | 2.75 cts | 2.5 cts | 2.25 cts |

| 2 cts | 1.88 cts | 1.75 cts | 1.63 cts | 1.5 cts |

| 1.38 cts | 1.25 cts | 1.13 cts | 1 ct | 0.88 cts | 0.75 cts |

| 0.63 cts | 0.5 cts | 0.38 cts | 0.25 cts | 0.13 cts | 0.06 cts |

A selection of gems

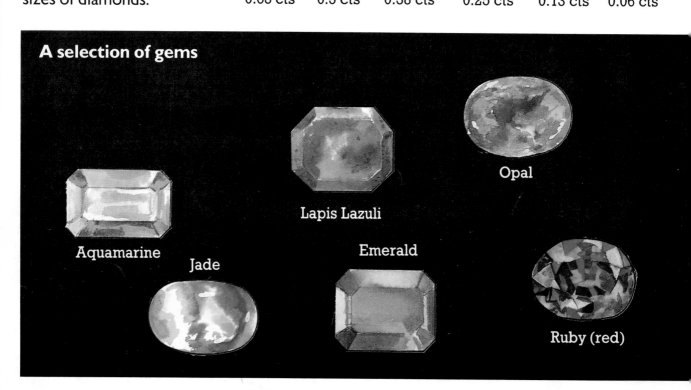

Aquamarine

Jade

Lapis Lazuli

Opal

Emerald

Ruby (red)

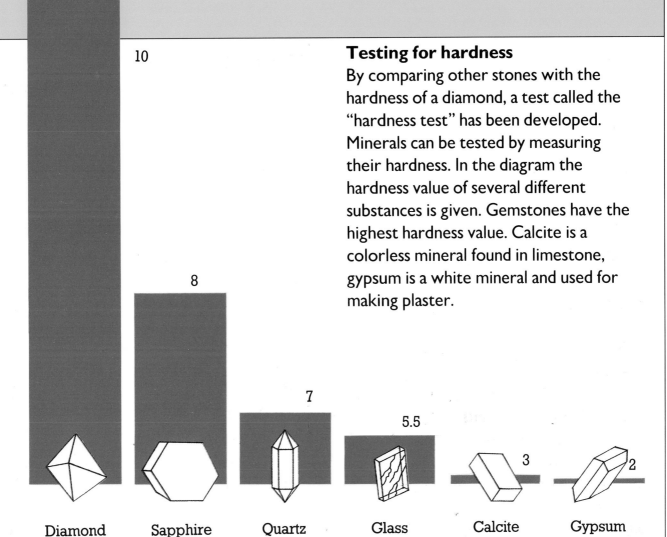

10

8

7

5.5

3

2

Diamond   Sapphire   Quartz   Glass   Calcite   Gypsum

Testing for hardness

By comparing other stones with the hardness of a diamond, a test called the "hardness test" has been developed. Minerals can be tested by measuring their hardness. In the diagram the hardness value of several different substances is given. Gemstones have the highest hardness value. Calcite is a colorless mineral found in limestone, gypsum is a white mineral and used for making plaster.

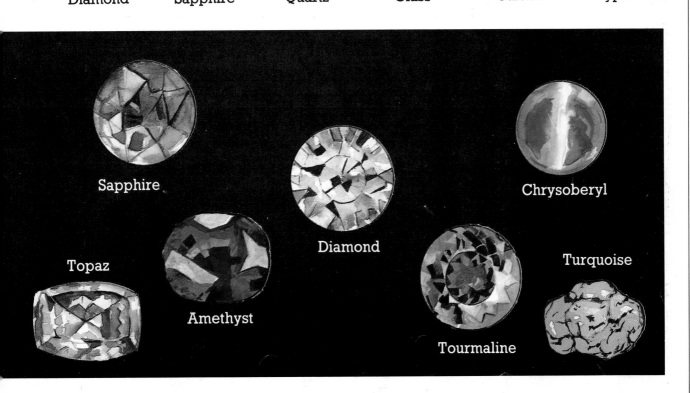

Sapphire

Chrysoberyl

Topaz

Diamond

Turquoise

Amethyst

Tourmaline

GLOSSARY

Artificial
Man-made. Not natural. Some substances, like diamond, ruby or quartz, can be made artificially although they are also found naturally. When this sort of substance is artificial we call it synthetic.

Carat
Gems are weighed in carats (ct). There are 5 ct in one gram.

Cat's-eyes and stars
Cabochon cut gems which show a line of light, or a criss-cross of lines, when a beam of light shines onto them. The lines move when the gem is tilted.

Crystal
A substance made with a neat, orderly pattern of atoms. This inner neatness sometimes causes crystals to have "faces" on the outside surface.

CZ
Cubic zirconia. A hard form of zirconium oxide crystal used as a diamond imitation. This is an artificial gem.

Fire
Colorful twinkling of a gem. The more a gem reflects light inside, from facet to facet, and the more it splits that light into a rainbow of colors, the more fire it displays.

INDEX

PRINTED IN BELGIUM BY
proost
INTERNATIONAL BOOK PRODUCTION